PIVOT POINT

PIVOT POINT FUNDAMENTALS: COSMETOLOGY
WIGS & HAIR ADDITIONS

1st Edition
4th Printing, October 2021
Printed in China

Pivot Point International, Inc.
Global Headquarters
8725 West Higgins Road, Suite 700
Chicago, IL 60631 USA

847-866-0500
pivot-point.com

13

13

2

CONTENTS

109ᶜ // WIGS & HAIR ADDITIONS

Have you ever wondered what you would do if you lost some or all of your hair? What options would you have to improve your situation?

WIG THEORY

109ᶜ.1

INSPIRE //

As a hair designer who uses wigs, you will have the power to help people regain their self-confidence after hair loss and satisfy clients who want an exciting or daring change.

ACHIEVE //

Following this lesson on *Wig Theory*, you'll be able to:

>> List the reasons clients wear wigs

>> State the different materials used in the composition of wigs

>> Explain the J and L Color Ring used for wigs

>> Describe the two general categories used to classify the construction of wigs and hairpieces

>> Compare the three methods used to attach hair or fiber to the wig cap or base

FOCUS //

WIG THEORY

History of Wigs

Composition, Colors and Construction

109ᶜ.1 | WIG THEORY

With knowledge about wigs, you will have the ability to empower people after hair loss and meet the needs of clients who desire a change. Maybe you have always wanted to help cancer patients who have experienced hair loss following medical treatments, or wanted to work with the community theater. The study of wigs will help you do all of this and much more.

DISCOVER**MORE**

Actress Raquel Welch is the Creative Director for the wig line Hair U Wear®, which has donated millions of dollars in wigs to the American Cancer Society® for women with cancer-related hair loss. The examples shown here were personally chosen by Welch for inclusion in her signature collection. Note the natural effects of the color designs and the softness and fluidity of the haircuts. Whether your clients just want to change their look or need to wear a wig for prescriptive purposes, wigs that look this real make it easier than ever before to offer this service with confidence.

HISTORY OF WIGS

Wigs are artificial hair items designed to cover the entire head. Men and women have worn them for both aesthetic and practical reasons for as long as history has been recorded. Wigs have risen and fallen in popularity according to trends, fashions and even politics. Below are examples of when wigs have been used in history.

» Ancient Egyptians began to wear wigs to protect their heads from the heat of the sun.

» Originally worn by the upper classes, wigs were eventually worn by all levels of Egyptian society, other than priests and laborers.

» The Romans and the Greeks wore wigs to varying degrees, depending on the fashions and customs of the moment.

» Several centuries later, during the Elizabethan era, the aristocracy sported curled wigs generously studded with precious gems.

» The extraordinary height and complexity of wig designs were, in many ways, indications of the extremes that led to the French Revolution.

» The prevailing trends, regardless of the extravagant expense and effort, were still followed by those who wished to maintain their status as fashion-conscious members of the aristocracy.

» During the 1950s and 1960s, wigs and hairpieces rose tremendously in popularity.

» The development of synthetic fibers, known as modacrylics, made mass production and lower prices possible.

» Wigs were worn as fashion accessories—especially in the evening—with no social stigma.

» Wigs have also been worn by actors and actresses throughout the ages.

» Theatrical wig making, especially of period designs, for theater and opera stages is an art form in itself.

The advances in technology and design have made it so much easier for you and your clients to take advantage of the wide range of wigs available.

COMPOSITION, COLORS AND CONSTRUCTION

Before performing wig services for your clients, it is important to have a good understanding of the composition, colors and construction of wigs.

WIG COMPOSITION

Wigs and hairpieces are composed of one or more of the following:

1. Human Hair	Generally made from Asian, Indian or European hair	
	Indian hair is wavy; Asian hair is straight; European hair is finer, straight hair	
	Hair is specially treated to protect against possible damage from styling services	
	Preferred by those wanting the most versatility	
	Most expensive; the supply of human hair is limited	
2. Synthetic Hair (Modacrylic)	Formulated from petroleum products	
	Produced as very long threads (monofilaments), which are then rolled onto spools	
	Cost-effective and efficient way to produce wigs	
	Available in unlimited shades	
	May not always resemble human hair but modern technology has produced very realistic results	
3. Animal Hair	Made most often of yak, angora, horse, camel or sheep hair	
	Even less resemblance to human hair than synthetic fibers	
	Most often used to produce theatrical wigs or wigs meant to be worn by display mannequins	

One of the highest grades of human hair used in wigs is referred to as Remy hair, which is hair with the cuticle intact and facing the same direction. Examples of synthetic fibers used in wigs are modacrylic, nylon or polyester.

If you're not certain whether a wig is made of human hair or synthetic (modacrylic) fiber, pull out several strands and hold them over a match flame. **A human hairstrand will burn slowly and produce an odor. A synthetic fiber will either "ball up" on the end (melt) and extinguish itself or burn very rapidly and produce no odor.**

WIG COLORS
J and L Color Ring

A color system called the J and L Color Ring is used by manufacturers to determine hair colors for wigs and hairpieces. The J and L Color Ring consists of 70 standardized colors.

» Contains numbered samples from black to palest blond

» Allows manufacturers to select from a variety of colors and create special effects such as highlighting

J and L Color Ring

SALONCONNECTION

Wig Sales and Services

Salons take many different approaches when it comes to wigs. Some salons choose to specialize in wig sales and services, while others may not sell wigs but offer cutting and styling services for them. Some salons may only provide recommendations for where clients may go to purchase or receive wig services.

WIG CONSTRUCTION

Wig construction falls into two general categories:

Cap Wigs	Consist of an elasticized mesh-fiber base to which the hair fiber is attached
	Available in several sizes and are produced most often as hand-tied wigs
Capless Wigs 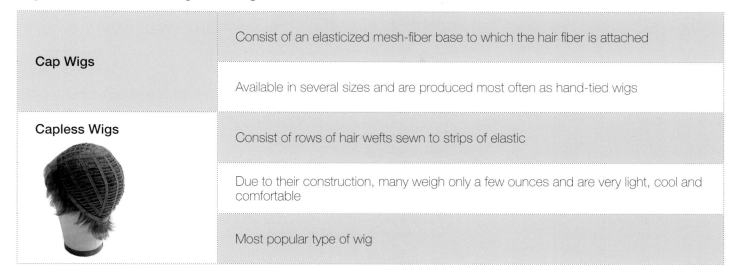	Consist of rows of hair wefts sewn to strips of elastic
	Due to their construction, many weigh only a few ounces and are very light, cool and comfortable
	Most popular type of wig

Inside of fabric glue / fabric wig cap

Hair and/or synthetic fibers may be attached to the wig cap or base in one of three methods:

1. **Hand-tied (hand-knotted)**

   » Produced by actually tying strands of hair by hand into a fine meshwork or foundation.

   » The patterns used simulate natural growth patterns that closely resemble human hair growth and create a natural look.

   » The hair is attached at close intervals and generally duplicates the density of a fairly thick head of human hair.

   » Since this process is labor-intensive and time-consuming, these wigs tend to be the most expensive.

2. **Machine-made**

   » **Consist of hair fiber sewn into long strips called wefts**, which are then sewn to the cap of the wig in a circular or crisscross pattern.

   » The hair direction is determined by the position in which the weft is sewn to the cap, making it difficult to perform design services.

3. **Semi-hand-tied**

   » Combinations of hand-tied and machine-made wigs.

   » Wigs are semi-hand-tied to create sturdy, natural-looking, reasonably priced hair replacements.

When helping your client select a wig, the wig's construction is significant in determining the best value in the client's price range.

» Capless wigs or caps that allow the scalp to "breathe" prevent excessive perspiration that may cause odors.

   ▪ These wigs need to be cleaned less frequently.

» Another factor of importance is that many wigs have flesh-colored sections designed to look like human skin.

   ▪ These sections give a realistic look when the hair is parted or moves.

   ▪ Hand-tied mesh is delicate and should be handled with care.

Wigs are an interesting and creative way to help clients who struggle with hair loss or are looking to try something new.

LESSONS LEARNED

The reasons that clients wear wigs include:

» Trends and fashion

» Quick, temporary appearance change

» Hair loss

» Theatrical presentations

The different materials used in wigs include:

» Human hair

» Synthetic fibers

» Animal hair

Wigs are standardized according to the 70 colors on the J and L Color Ring, which are numbered from black to palest blond.

The two general categories used to classify the construction of wigs and hairpieces include:

» Cap wigs that have a mesh-fiber base to which fibers are attached

» Capless wigs that have rows of wefts sewn onto elastic strips

The three methods used to attach hair and/or synthetic fiber to the wig cap or base are:

» Hand-tied, which consists of actually tying strands of hair by hand into a fine meshwork or foundation

» Machine-made, which consists of hair fibers sewn into long strips called wefts, which are then sewn to the cap of the wig in a circular, straight or crisscross pattern

» Semi-hand-tied, which is produced using the combined methods of hand-tied and machine-made wigs

WIG SERVICES

EXPLORE //

Have you ever seen someone with a wig and wondered if the wig came that way or if it had to be styled? Where does someone go to get their wig styled?

109ᶜ.2

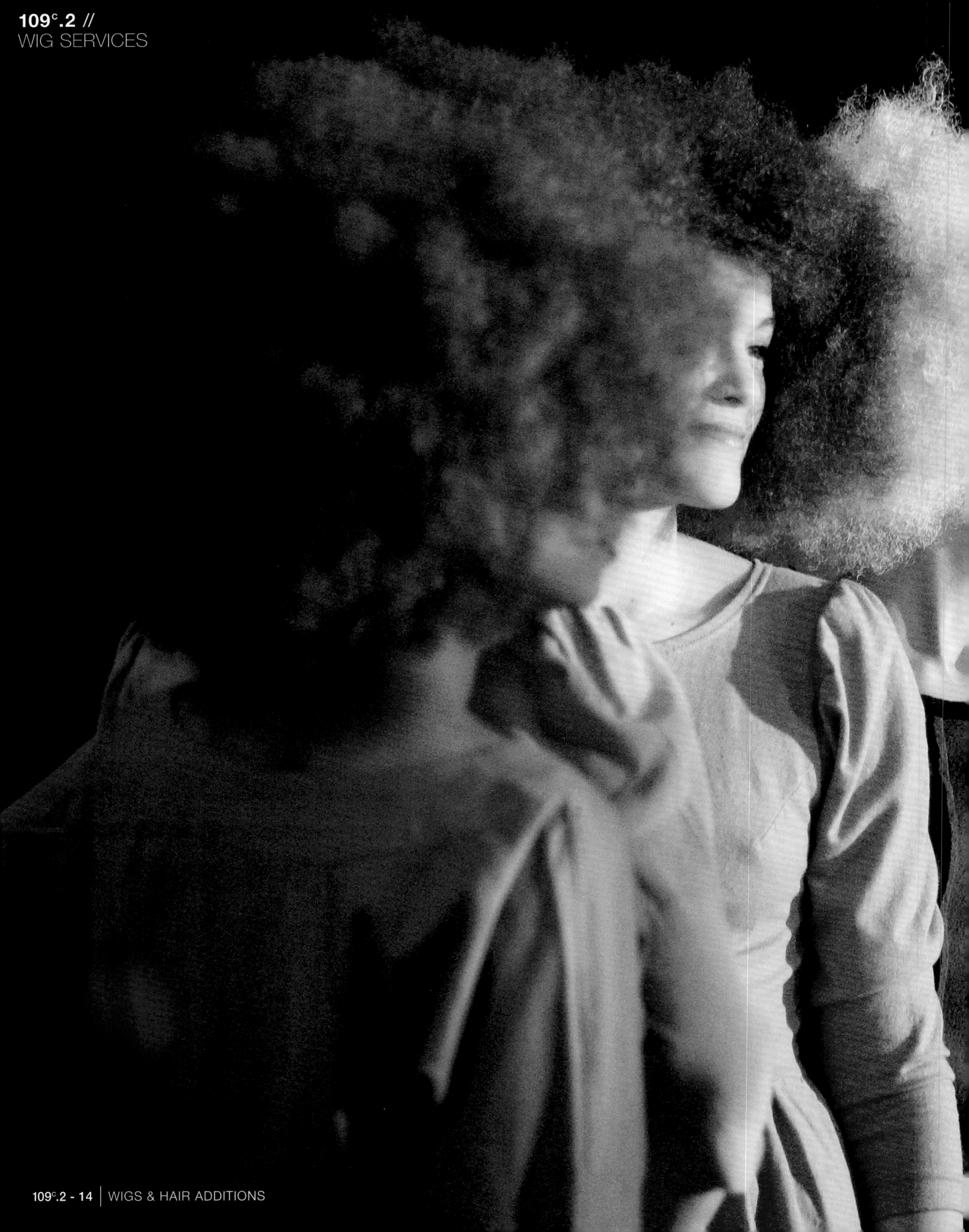

INSPIRE //

Understanding how to provide customized wig services for your clients will help build a reputation as a wig advisor or expert.

Following this lesson on *Wig Services*, you'll be able to:

ACHIEVE //

>> List points to keep in mind when communicating with a client for a wig service

>> State different wig services you can offer a client

>> Summarize the differences between cleaning and conditioning a human-hair wig versus a synthetic wig

>> Explain different techniques and tips for cutting and shaping a wig

FOCUS //

WIG SERVICES

Wig Measurement and Fitting

Wig Cleaning and Styling

109ᶜ.2 | WIG SERVICES

Wigs provide a wide range of solutions and fashion statements for you and your clients. Your client has taken a big step by purchasing a wig, and you can help them feel at ease by personalizing the wig to fit each individual need.

Regardless of the reason(s) that the client desires a wig service, discretion is always important. Whether hair loss is hereditary or caused by illness or medication, many clients will be very self-conscious about their need to seek your services. Keep the following in mind when communicating with a client for wig services:

>> Ensure client comfort by providing a private area for wig fitting.

>> The client needs to trust you as the salon professional.

>> Be especially sympathetic and emotionally supportive, because you will often be dealing with the adverse conditions that cause hair loss.

>> Discuss with your client certain design options that may make it easier to attain realistic-looking results.

>> Much of the client's comfort level with the service and the wig itself will be determined during your conversation with the client.

>> Serve your client with dignity, respect and a positive, supportive attitude.

WIG MEASUREMENT AND FITTING

Helping your clients choose the appropriate wig includes confirming the wig is comfortable and fits properly. This important step will help your client to feel confident whenever the wig is worn. Taking appropriate measurements, especially if you are ordering direct from the manufacturer, saves time and prevents returns.

It's also best practice to teach your client how to position their wig on their head. Your client will be more likely to duplicate the look you achieve in the salon, and will thank you for the lesson.

WIG MEASUREMENT

In order for your client's wig to fit comfortably, you have to properly measure the wig to your client's head size and shape. Although wig manufacturers may require additional, specific measurements for their products, following these basic measurement guidelines will help you properly fit the majority of wigs for your clients.

Ready-to-Wear Wig Measurements

If you are ordering a ready-to-wear wig, the only measurement you will need is the circumference.

» *Brush the client's hair smooth. If the hair is long, pin it flat.*

» *Measure the circumference of the head.*
  - *Begin at the middle of the front hairline and circle the entire head.*
  - *Run the tape just above the ear, around the back and return to the starting point.*
  - *Be sure the client's ears are not caught under the tape measure.*
  - *The average hairline circumference is 22" (55.8 cm).*

Custom-Made Wig Measurements

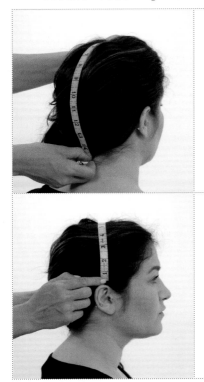

When ordering a custom wig or making adjustments, you will measure the circumference as shown above and also the following:

Front to back:

» *Measure the distance from the center of the front hairline, over the crown, to the center of the nape hairline.*

» *For the most comfortable fit, bend the client's head back to find the spot at the base of the skull where the wig will rest.*

» *Measure the distance from ear to ear over the apex or top of the head.*

Most wigs are made in an Average cap size, but some will be offered in Petite, Petite/Average, Average, Average/Large and Large.

PUTTING ON A WIG

Along with selecting and/or creating the perfect wig for your client, it is important to teach your client the easiest way to put on a wig. This will help the client feel more comfortable wearing the wig and eliminate frustrations.

Putting on a Wig: Guidelines

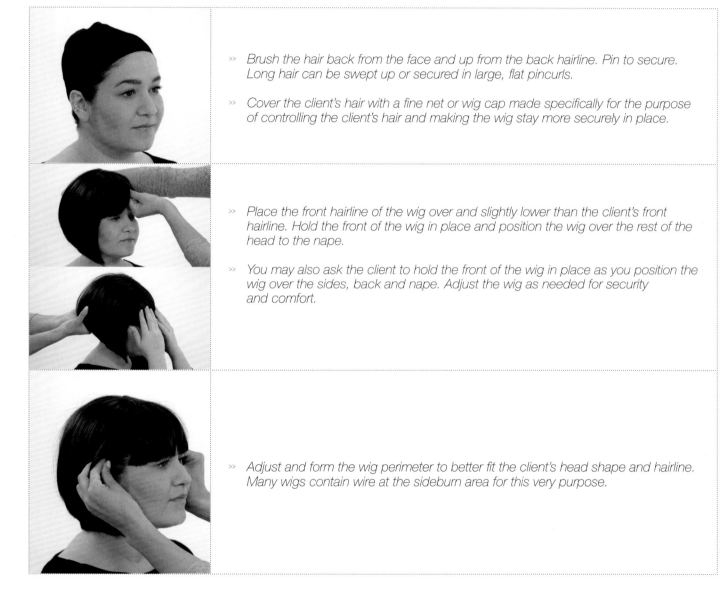

>> *Brush the hair back from the face and up from the back hairline. Pin to secure. Long hair can be swept up or secured in large, flat pincurls.*

>> *Cover the client's hair with a fine net or wig cap made specifically for the purpose of controlling the client's hair and making the wig stay more securely in place.*

>> *Place the front hairline of the wig over and slightly lower than the client's front hairline. Hold the front of the wig in place and position the wig over the rest of the head to the nape.*

>> *You may also ask the client to hold the front of the wig in place as you position the wig over the sides, back and nape. Adjust the wig as needed for security and comfort.*

>> *Adjust and form the wig perimeter to better fit the client's head shape and hairline. Many wigs contain wire at the sideburn area for this very purpose.*

WIG BLOCKING

When performing wig services such as designing or cleaning, it is important that the size and shape of the wig not be compromised. Proper sizing procedures, called blocking, will help maintain the wig's original size. Canvas-covered head forms, called wig blocks, are manufactured for use during these services.

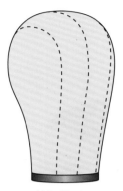

Wig Block

>> The blocks are available in six sizes: 20″, 20.5″, 21″, 21.5″, 22″ and 22.5″ (50, 51.25, 52.5, 53.75, 55 and 56.25 cm).

>> One of these sizes should closely match the circumference measurement of the client's head.

>> If the wig needs to be stretched, it is placed on a block larger than the client's head.

>> If the wig needs to be shrunk, it is placed on a smaller block.

>> The block is placed on a swivel clamp for control.

Wig Blocking Guidelines

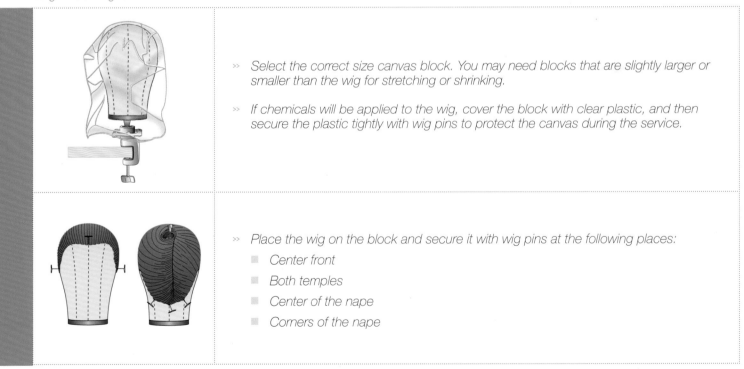

>> *Select the correct size canvas block. You may need blocks that are slightly larger or smaller than the wig for stretching or shrinking.*

>> *If chemicals will be applied to the wig, cover the block with clear plastic, and then secure the plastic tightly with wig pins to protect the canvas during the service.*

>> *Place the wig on the block and secure it with wig pins at the following places:*
- *Center front*
- *Both temples*
- *Center of the nape*
- *Corners of the nape*

CUSTOMIZING OR FITTING A WIG

Custom-ordered wigs can be quite expensive and, therefore, cost-prohibitive for many clients. Fortunately, the majority of clients will be able to use a ready-to-wear wig, one that will not require any adjustments or alterations from a salon professional. However, if adjustments or alterations are necessary, you will want to be able to offer this service to your clients.

The following adjustments are useful when the wig needs a slight change:

>> Elastic bands through the nape or crown, at the bottom back or at either side of the nape allow for easy adjustments.

>> Elastic bands are adjusted by one of the following methods:

- Using small strips of Velcro®

- Securing with small hooks

- Removing stitches from elastic that has been sewn to the cap

>> The elastic band itself may need to be replaced occasionally or secured in place by sewing it down.

The following alterations are used when a greater change is needed in the wig:

» **Darts are alterations made vertically to remove width in the nape area (from ear to ear).**

» **Tucks are alterations made horizontally to shorten a wig from the front hairline to the nape.**

  ▪ Horizontal alterations are usually made with the tuck near the crown to avoid excess bulk close to the perimeter.

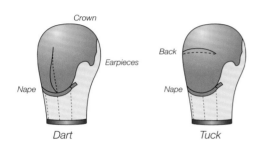

These adjustment and alteration techniques are considered customization, and additional training is recommended.

STRETCHING OR SHRINKING CAP WIGS

In some instances, you will be able to adjust the size of a wig without making tucks or darts, by either stretching or shrinking the wig. You might need to stretch a wig if it is just a little too tight or if it has somehow shrunk a bit.

Stretching Cap Wig: Guidelines

» Select a block one size larger than the wig's circumference.

» Turn the wig inside out and thoroughly moisten the cap of the wig by spraying with hot water.

» Turn the wig right-side out and carefully stretch it over a wig block one size larger than the circumference of the wig itself.

» Secure the wig to the block along the hairline using wig pins.

» Design the hair if desired and allow the wig to dry. Dry the wig under a warm dryer only if the wig is human hair; heat can distort curl patterns of synthetic fibers.

Shrinking Cap Wig: Guidelines

» Select a block one size smaller than the wig's circumference.

» Turn the wig inside out and thoroughly moisten the cap of the wig by spraying with hot water.

» Turn the wig right-side out and place it over a wig block one size smaller than the circumference of the wig itself.

» Secure the wig to the block along the hairline using wig pins.

» Design the hair if desired and allow the wig to dry. Dry the wig under a warm dryer only if the wig is human hair; heat can distort curl patterns of synthetic fibers.

WIG CLEANING AND STYLING
CLEANING AND CONDITIONING

Many wig manufacturers will give you guidelines for cleaning and conditioning their wigs. Some manufacturers also have specific products available that you can offer your clients. Regardless of the specific brand of products, the following information will serve you well as you work with your clients' wigs.

Cleaning Human-Hair Wigs

>> Human-hair wigs should be cleaned every 2-4 weeks, depending on how frequently the piece is worn.

>> Human-hair wigs should be conditioned following each cleaning, since some wig-cleansing products, like liquid dry-cleaning shampoos, can be very drying.

Cleaning Synthetic-Hair Wigs

>> Synthetic wigs do not require cleaning as frequently as their human-hair counterparts.

>> Synthetic conditioning sprays are recommended to keep the fibers in optimum condition.

>> Synthetic wigs do not require conditioning as human-hair wigs do.

Human-Hair Wigs: Cleaning and Conditioning Guidelines

Since hand-tied wigs generally have a delicate construction and are more expensive, extra care needs to be taken in their cleaning.

>> Gently remove tangles with fingers or a wide-tooth comb. Do NOT brush.

>> Run cool water in the direction of hair until wet.

>> Place a quarter-sized amount of shampoo in the palm of your hand, then distribute through the hair from top to bottom.

>> Run cool water in the direction of hair until water runs clear.

>> Press and squeeze water out, then towel-blot excess.

>> Spray leave-in conditioner, avoiding knots or base.

>> Conditioner should be applied from midshaft to ends. Avoid conditioner close to the base and knots.

Synthetic-Hair Wigs: Cleaning Guidelines

» Gently remove tangles with fingers or a wide-tooth comb. Do NOT brush.

» Run cool water in the direction of the hair until wet.

» Place a quarter-sized amount of shampoo in the palm of your hand, then distribute through the hair from top to bottom.

» Run cool water in the direction of the hair until water runs clear.

» Rinse thoroughly, paying attention to the inside of the cap, as well as the hair.

» Press and squeeze water out, then towel-blot excess.

» Spray synthetic fiber leave-in conditioner.

» Place on folding wig stand to dry or use a blow dryer on a very low setting.

Shampoos and conditioners specifically designed for synthetic wigs are available from wig manufacturers.

DISCOVER**MORE**

Often a variety of different names will be given to the same service. Discover the names in your market area by contacting the salons that offer wig services and asking them what they call each service. Ask them about pricing too. You'll find that not only do names change, but pricing will vary between establishments also. Share your findings for an interesting classroom discussion.

COLORING SERVICES

Although most wig manufacturers can custom color their wigs and hairpieces in almost any shade you can imagine, it is an extra benefit to your clients if you can offer this service to them in cases where a desired color doesn't exist for their particular choice.

>> Color should not be applied to synthetic wigs, since the nonporous fiber will not allow the hair shaft to be coated or penetrated.

>> Human-hair wigs can be effectively colored with temporary rinses that last from shampoo to shampoo, semi-permanent colors, fillers or low-level (darker) oxidative colors.

>> Human-hair wigs have already been chemically treated, so it's advisable to avoid oxidative colors that lighten the hair and lighteners, since it may be hard to predict the results.

>> Before coloring a wig, be sure to perform a strand test.

>> Keep color off the wig cap as much as possible, since color may eventually dissolve the fabric.

Human-Hair Wigs: Coloring Guidelines

>> Clean the wig following the Cleaning and Conditioning Guidelines.

>> Apply the appropriate color on the wig hair according to product directions. Take thin partings and use an angled brush, carefully avoiding the cap. Allow the color to process and remain on the hair according to manufacturer's instructions.

>> Remove the color and condition hair.

>> Apply desired styling products and set the hair with rollers, or distribute hair in the desired direction and allow the wig to dry.

CUTTING AND SHAPING

The majority of wigs are available "precut." The hair or fiber is attached to the cap so that the resulting length arrangement creates a finished design. Keep in mind, though, that human-hair wigs are more likely to require a full shaping than their synthetic counterparts.

>> Most wigs are produced with about twice as much hair as is on an average human head.

>> It is often necessary to taper or thin a wig in order to decrease bulk and create a more natural-looking appearance.

   ▪ You may use a razor or thinning shears to thin a human-hair wig.

   ▪ It is not recommended to use a razor on synthetic wigs, since they tend to frizz easily.

   ▪ Thinning is often needed to remove bulk, especially near the front hairline and behind the ears.

>> Be sure to cut synthetic fiber when it is dry to avoid additional frizzing.

>> Be especially careful to avoid cutting into the cap or the wefting.

>> On a hand-tied wig, be sure that the knotting remains secure. Do not cut any of the knots.

>> You may need to do some customizing on a precut wig so that it perfectly suits your client's features.

   ▪ The fringe and front hairline are common areas that require customizing.

   ▪ Thinning or tapering may also be performed closer to the hair ends as needed.

>> If a full haircut, or sculpture is required, it is best to establish the length and basic lines while the client is wearing the wig so you can relate to your client's facial features.

>> Chin straps are helpful to prevent a wig from slipping on your client's head while you are cutting.

>> Moving the wig to a block after the basic lines have been established will simplify the remaining blending and shaping efforts by allowing you more movement and control.

   ▪ Make sure the wig is properly positioned and secured to the block before cutting.

   ▪ If you add a fringe or bang to a wig, rub the knots to redirect the fiber forward. Use a blow dryer on a low setting to shape and redirect synthetic hair.

1. Customize the fringe.

2. Blend and shape.

3. Ensure positioning.

Hairline Tip

Backcombing the hair very close to the front hairline of the wig can help you soften the hairline and create a more natural-looking result.

SETTING AND FINISHING

HUMAN-HAIR WIGS
Can be either wet-set or set when dry

SYNTHETIC-HAIR WIGS
Are pre-designed with predetermined curl patterns

>> *Setting a human-hair wig is very much like setting the hair growing on a human head.*

>> *Particular attention should be paid to creating closer shapes at the nape and making sure the hairline is covered.*

>> *Pincurls can be used where closeness is required.*

>> *Wig pins can be used on the block instead of picks to hold rollers or pincurls in place.*

>> *This curl pattern is not intended to be altered by the client or the salon professional.*

>> *The predetermined curl patterns in synthetic wigs require only minimal designing after cleaning.*

>> *Stay aware of manufacturers' advancements in synthetic fibers.*

>> *Some manufacturers now offer newer heat-friendly synthetic fiber that can withstand up to 350° Fahrenheit/176° Celsius. Be very cautious and always follow the manufacturer's instructions.*

Alert!
Don't put synthetic wigs under a dryer, since excessive heat can melt the fiber.

Being familiar with best practices when it comes to a variety of wig services will make your clients comfortable and increase their confidence in you as a salon professional.

LESSONS LEARNED

>> Some points to keep in mind when communicating with a client for a wig service are:

- Ensure client comfort by providing a private area for wig fitting.

- The client needs to trust you as the salon professional.

- Be especially sympathetic and emotionally supportive.

- Discuss with your client certain design options that may make it easier to attain realistic-looking results.

- Much of the client's comfort level with the service and the wig itself will be determined during your conversation with the client.

- Serve your client with dignity, respect and a positive, supportive attitude.

>> Only the circumference is required to fit a ready-to-wear wig. Custom-made wigs may require forehead-to-nape and ear-to-ear measurements.

>> Human-hair wigs require shampooing every 2-4 weeks depending on how often they are worn. Human-hair wigs should be conditioned following each cleaning. Avoid conditioner in knots —apply midstrand to ends.

>> Synthetic wigs need a conditioning spray to keep the fibers in good condition.

>> Hair color should not be applied to synthetic wigs.

>> Human-hair wigs can be colored effectively with temporary, semi-permanent and low-level oxidative hair colors. Avoid getting product on base of wig.

>> Techniques and tips for cutting a wig include:

- Taper or thin a wig in order to decrease bulk and create a more natural-looking appearance.

- Use a razor or thinning shears to thin a human-hair wig.

- Avoid using a razor on synthetic wigs, since they tend to frizz easily.

- Thinning may be needed to remove bulk, especially near the front hairline and behind the ears.

- Sculpt synthetic fiber when it is dry to avoid additional frizzing.

- Setting techniques can be performed on human-hair wigs.

- Avoid heat on synthetic fiber —unless the manufacturer has approved a heat setting.

H 109ᶜ.3

AIRPIECES AND HAIR ADDITIONS

INSPIRE //

Hairpiece and hair addition services provide fun alternatives and fill special needs with the endless options they provide.

FOCUS //

HAIRPIECES AND HAIR ADDITIONS

Hairpiece and Hair Addition Fibers

Hairpieces

Hair Addition Methods

Hairpiece and Hair Addition Service Essentials

Think of the entertainment industry. How do celebrities change their hair color, length and even texture so often?

ACHIEVE //

Following this lesson on *Hairpieces and Hair Additions*, you'll be able to:

» Identify three types of fiber used in hairpieces and hair additions

» List the different types of hairpieces and where they are most likely positioned

» Compare strand-by-strand to weft hair additions

» Explain why additional care is required during a hairpiece or hair addition consultation

109ᶜ.3 | HAIRPIECES AND HAIR ADDITIONS

Hairpieces and hair additions offer solutions to a wide variety of alternative hair needs. Manufacturers continue to provide technology improvements, making it easier for professionals to create extremely natural-looking results.

Hairpieces consist of a man-made base with attached hair or fiber. Hairpieces are integrated with your client's own hair to:

» Cover areas of hair loss or sparseness

» Create a special-occasion design

» Make a quick change, just for fun

Hair additions consist of loose hair fiber or wefts designed to be attached to the base of the client's own hair. Hair additions are also called hair extensions, and they can be attached all over the head, or to specific areas to add any or all of the following:

» Length

» Density

» Texture

» Color

HAIRPIECE AND HAIR ADDITION FIBERS

Hairpieces and hair additions can be constructed of human hair, synthetic fiber or animal hair.

Human Hair	» Most expensive, especially longer lengths
	» Replicates the most natural look » Styling with heat and hair coloring is possible
	» Remy hair is one of the highest grades of human hair; the cuticle is intact and facing in one direction, resulting in less tangling
	» Requires ongoing care and maintenance
Synthetic Fiber	» Cost-effective and efficient
	» Formulated from petroleum products; made with nylon and polyester
	» Produced as very long threads (monofilaments), which are rolled onto spools and cut at appropriate lengths
	» Color and curl patterns almost unlimited
	» Limited styling change possible, no color change » Newer fibers accept low styling heat; check with manufacturer first » Easily maintained
Animal Hair	» Less expensive than human hair
	» Sources include yak, camel, angora, horse and sheep
	» Less resemblance to human hair than synthetic fibers » Some change in texture and color is possible » Used to produce fantasy hairpieces

If you're ever unsure which fiber you're working with, light it. Human hair burns; synthetic hair melts.

HAIRPIECES

Hairpieces are often categorized or named according to the purpose of the piece and where it is designed to be worn. Manufacturers update these names to follow marketing trends. The chart below identifies several classic names that are very common.

TYPES OF HAIRPIECES

BANG	Shorter wefts of hair, sometimes hand-tied, designed to clip in and create a fringe over the forehead
CASCADE	Longer lengths attached to an oblong-shaped dome base to create special effects
CHIGNON	Fairly long segment of looped hair, preformed into a specific shape and worn at the crown or at the nape
FALL	Longer lengths attached to a base that covers the crown, occipital and nape
PONY	Long lengths grouped together, also called a switch, designed to quickly clip in and simulate a ponytail
TOUPÉE	Hairpiece designed to be worn on top of the head to cover bald or thinning hair
WIGLET	Shorter hair, 6" (15.2 cm) or less, attached to a round, flat base and used to create fullness or height at the top and crown areas

HAIRPIECE ATTACHMENTS

Hairpieces can be attached with combs, clips, integration and adhesives. Choice often depends on the size of the hairpiece and how long the client will be wearing it. Sometimes a hairpiece has a combination of attachments.

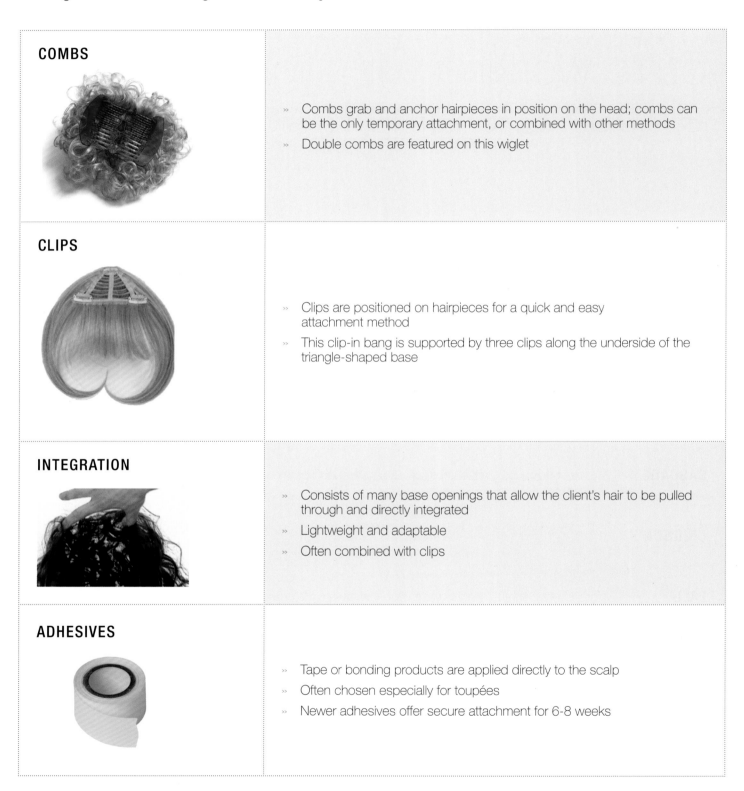

COMBS

» Combs grab and anchor hairpieces in position on the head; combs can be the only temporary attachment, or combined with other methods

» Double combs are featured on this wiglet

CLIPS

» Clips are positioned on hairpieces for a quick and easy attachment method

» This clip-in bang is supported by three clips along the underside of the triangle-shaped base

INTEGRATION

» Consists of many base openings that allow the client's hair to be pulled through and directly integrated

» Lightweight and adaptable

» Often combined with clips

ADHESIVES

» Tape or bonding products are applied directly to the scalp

» Often chosen especially for toupées

» Newer adhesives offer secure attachment for 6-8 weeks

TOUPÉES

Toupées are hairpieces designed to cover hair loss and thinning on top of the head. Manufacturers now offer systems with natural hairlines so thin no one would suspect a client is wearing a piece. Clients who wear toupées need well-trained professionals.

If you choose to offer these profitable services in the future, seek additional training to ensure you know how to:

» Recommend and select the correct toupée design and size

» Cut and blend the system to ensure natural-looking results

» Schedule regular and ongoing service appointments

Before *After*

A solution to thinning hair and hair loss is appreciated by men of all ages and hair types.

HAIR ADDITION METHODS

Hair additions fall into two main classifications:

1. **Strand-by-Strand** – Loose or prepared strands of hair or fiber that are added to natural hair along attachment points. Design patterns and the density of strand placement are unlimited.

2. **Wefts** – Strands of hair or fiber that have been sewn or bonded along one edge and added to natural hair along attachment lines. Patterns of placement include attaching wefts along horizontal, diagonal or curved partings or tracks.

STRAND-BY-STRAND/POINTS

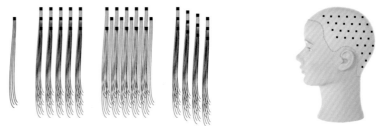

WEFTS/LINES

To keep attachments hidden, successful patterns avoid positioning hair additions too close to the surface of the head or to the perimeter hairline.

STRAND-BY-STRAND METHODS

Attachment methods for strand-by-strand additions include:

» Clip-in

» Thermal fusion

» Cold fusion

» Beading/tubing

» Braiding

Clip-in, sewn or glued hair addition strands are a simple way to add a temporary accent of color or texture just for fun. Human hair and heat-friendly synthetic strands can be curled along with the natural hair.

Thermal Fusion

Thermal fusion methods of hair addition involve applying heat to melt or bond the addition to natural hair. Additions are tipped on one end with a bonding product. Heat is applied with tong-like tools to activate the bond and attach the addition to small sections of the client's hair. When you design the attachment pattern, make sure you observe and follow your client's natural growth pattern. Attaching strands against the natural growth pattern will cause discomfort for the client, and possible damage to her hair.

After

Before

Thermal fusion hair addition services require a full system, which includes specially designed pre-tipped strands, and the related fusion machine, from the chosen manufacturer.

STEPS FOR STRAND-BY-STRAND FUSION

Select small rectangular sections of natural hair within rows and isolate with a plastic disc.

Place hair addition strand behind the natural hair.

Apply heating element (tongs in this case) over both strands, until bonding agent has softened.

Use your fingers to roll bonded area until natural hair and hair addition are joined.

Reapply heating tool and roll again as needed.

Add color strands within the design to blend with client's natural hair.

Be creative, but consult with your client first. Choices are unlimited. Check out manufacturers' websites for ideas.

Fusion hair additions need to be removed during a professional salon service. It is important to share information about maintenance, including removal and reattachment, at the client's initial appointment. The process of removing thermal fusion hair additions requires softening the original bond and releasing the added hair. Removal methods correspond to the application method and are taught by the manufacturer.

Cold Fusion

The term **cold fusion** is used by manufacturers to refer to a variety of methods that attach hair without a thermal tool. One cold fusion method is similar to thermal fusion, but a special machine generates ultrasonic waves, or "vibration," to secure the bond. Other cold fusion methods incorporate beads or rings and specially designed pliers. Be sure to explore the pros and cons of each method.

Beading/Tubing

Beading and/or tubing methods use a thin loop to thread natural hair through a bead. Hair addition strands are then threaded into the bead. The bead is closed with a plier-like tool to link the addition and the natural hair. Various sizes and colors of beads or ring-like tubes are available, and some systems require heated tools or pliers.

SALON**CONNECTION**

Get Certified!

Professionals who provide strand-by-strand hair addition services must attend certification classes offered by the specific manufacturer whose hair addition system they use. These classes ensure professionals know the proper techniques and safety measures required for a successful hair addition service. Passing the certification assessment allows you to purchase the system and reorder hairstrands. Certifications are great for your resumé!

Braiding

Off-the-scalp braiding uses a standard 3-strand braiding technique to attach loose fiber or hair. The hair addition fiber or hair is incorporated along with the natural hair as it is braided. The ends can be left free, or if the addition is synthetic and extends beyond the natural hair, it can be fused with heat.

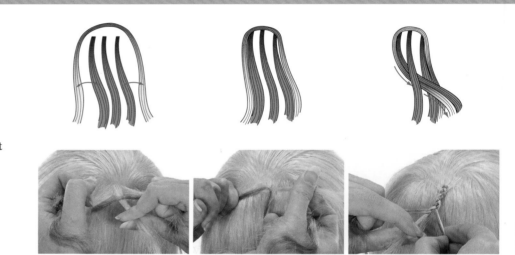

WEFT ATTACHMENT METHODS

Attachment methods for wefts include taping, clipping, bonding and track-and-sew.

Taping and Clipping

A weft designed for taping includes an edge with adhesive, used to adhere to the client's hair. A weft designed for clipping has small clips attached to its edge. Both taping and clipping are quick and easy attachment methods, designed for temporary changes.

Tape on and off

Clip in

Bonding

Two methods of bonding include 1) taping and 2) liquid adhesive. The first method combines the ease of taping small wefts with the security of bonding. These wefts feature double-adhesive edges with sticky sides to hold the weft in position before securing.

1. Create part and remove strip.

2. Position weft, release thin amount of natural hair above part.

3. Sandwich weft with natural hair above and below; fuse with tool to create the bond.

The second method, **liquid bonding**, is the attachment of additional hair fiber to a client's own hair with a glue adhesive. The adhesive is applied along partings of the client's hair and to the sewn edge of the weft before placing in position.

Since some clients may have an allergic reaction to ingredients in adhesives, it is necessary to perform a patch test prior to the direct application of these products.

STEPS FOR BONDING WEFTS WITH LIQUID ADHESIVE

» Create part, then measure length of weft to match and cut it accordingly.

» Ensure that both client's hair and weft are completely dry prior to performing the service.

» Apply liquid adhesive to hair along the parting.

» Ensure bond by applying the adhesive consistently.

» Apply adhesive along sewn edge of weft

  » Place weft along part

  » Apply gentle pressure along entire length of weft

» Advise client that longevity of this type of hair-addition service is influenced by:

  » Frequency of shampooing

  » Oiliness of scalp (oil will break down adhesive)

  » Daily products used

Clients should return to the salon for the removal of bonded wefts when their natural hair has grown no longer than 1" (2.5 cm). An adhesive removal solution, recommended by the manufacturer, is applied and allowed to penetrate the bond to loosen the weft. Always follow manufacturer's step-by-step instructions.

Track-and-Sew

The **track-and-sew** method incorporates 3-strand, on-the-scalp braids, which are used as a support structure to sew hair wefts onto.

Tracks, which are strips of hair that have been parted off to be braided, can be created to follow the curves of the head or in any straight line. Clean, precise tracks depend on clean, precise parting lines. Once you have parted the track, secure the remaining hair on either side out of the way.

» Plan your track so that the ends of the braids can be camouflaged by the sewn-on wefts.

» Position the tracks at least 1" (2.5 cm) behind the hairline so they are not visible.

» On finer or straighter hair, crimped fiber may be added to the braided track for stability.

Sewing Methods

Straight and/or curved needles with blunted ends are used to sew wefts to braided tracks. These blunted ends help avoid discomfort or injury to you or your client. Generally, a cotton/polyester blend thread is used.

OVERCAST STITCH

An overcast stitch is the simplest and quickest stitch used to secure a weft to a track.

»   Thread needle; make sure length of thread is double the length of weft/track.

»   Sew through weft first, and then bring needle through the track.

»   Pass needle and thread over and under.

»   Move slightly to one side to complete next stitch.

Use a lock stitch at either end of track for added security.

LOCK STITCH

Create a lock stitch by passing the needle inside the loop of thread before tightening.

Lock stitches can be used across the length of the entire weft/track. Space the stitches equally to distribute the weight evenly.

DOUBLE-LOCK STITCH

A double-lock stitch can be used to secure a weft at either end or across the length of the weft/track. Wind the thread around the needle twice to create a "double lock."

Sewn-in wefts need to be removed professionally. Section the hair to identify the weft and carefully place a seam ripper or scissors under the thread, taking care to cut only the thread and not the hair.

As you cut the thread, the weft will start to loosen along the track. Once all the thread is removed, the weft can be lifted from the hair. Gently remove the braided tracks, and then comb the hair. You will see some hair loss. This should only be natural hair loss, which was held in by the braid.

DISCOVER**MORE**

Keep an eye on consumer trends and industry advancements to learn about new designs in alternative hair and the latest attachment methods. Manufacturers' websites are an excellent resource to browse, and they will often include salons and studios that provide their brand of hairpieces and hair addition services. If your interest is piqued, consider stopping by a local salon or hair replacement studio to experience what they offer first-hand. Introduce yourself as a future professional, and ask to watch. It is good business to share. Who knows, you might recommend clients to them in the future, or decide to send them your resumé.

HAIRPIECE AND HAIR ADDITION SERVICE ESSENTIALS

There are several things to keep in mind when communicating with a client requesting a hairpiece or hair addition service:

» Provide a comfortable and private environment.

» Build trust by using professional language and discreet behavior.

» Observe and record details about hairlines, natural hair length, texture and color during the client consultation.

» Discuss various design options that may make it easier to attain desired results.

» Record the type of service performed and the price the client was charged.

» Advise the recommended interval between appointments, and clarify the price of follow-up services.

» Serve your client with dignity, respect and a positive, supportive attitude.

LESSONS LEARNED

Fibers used in the composition of hairpieces and hair additions include:

» Human hair

» Synthetic fibers

» Animal hair

Types of hairpieces and their positioning include:

» Bang – Forehead

» Cascade – Crown, center back

» Chignon – Nape or crown

» Fall – Top and back

» Pony – Top or nape

» Toupée – Top of head

» Wiglet – Top of head

There are two main categories of hair additions: strand-by-strand and weft.

Strand-by-strand hair additions produce points of attachment within the client's existing hair using:

» Clip-In – Clips are sewn or glued to hair addition strands

» Thermal Fusion – Fusing strands with client's hair with heat-activated bonding agent

» Cold Fusion – Attaches hair without a thermal tool

» Beading/Tubing – Attaches hair addition strands using beads/tubes

» Braiding – Incorporates loose hair fiber additions with natural hair

Wefts produce lines of attachment within client's existing hair using:

» Taping and Clipping – Simple positioning along a parting of natural hair

» Bonding – Securing wefts to client's hair with adhesive

» Track-and-Sew – Creating an on-the-scalp braid and sewing wefts to the braid

Discretion is critical when communicating and consulting with a client about hairpieces and hair addition services because a client's privacy and comfort are your responsibility.

WIG, HAIRPIECE AND HAIR

ADDITION ESSENTIALS | 109^c.4

If you were a wig maker, what new design or tool would you introduce to the industry?

INSPIRE //

Wig artistry plus working
smartly and safely is the
recipe for satisfied clients.

ACHIEVE //

Following this lesson on *Wig,
Hairpiece and Hair Addition
Essentials*, you'll be able to:

>> Identify the products, tools.
and supplies needed to
perform wig, hairpiece and
hair addition services

>> Recognize equipment used
in wig, hairpiece and hair
addition services

>> Summarize infection
control and safety
concerns before, during
and after a wig, hairpiece
or hair addition service

FOCUS //

**WIG, HAIRPIECE
AND HAIR ADDITION
ESSENTIALS**

Overview: Wig, Hairpiece and
Hair Addition Essentials

Wig, Hairpiece and Hair
Addition Infection Control
and Safety

109ᶜ.4 |
WIG, HAIRPIECE AND HAIR ADDITION ESSENTIALS

F or the wide range of possibilities that exist for wigs, hairpieces and hair additions, you will want to be familiar with the essentials needed to help you meet the needs of all clients.

OVERVIEW: WIG, HAIRPIECE AND HAIR ADDITION ESSENTIALS

In order to perform services related to wigs, hairpieces and hair additions, you will need to have a clear understanding of the products, tool, supply and equipment choices you will make as you work with each client.

WIG, HAIRPIECE AND HAIR ADDITION PRODUCTS

Refer to Safety Data Sheets (SDS) for all products used in the salon.

PRODUCTS	FUNCTION
Nonflammable Liquid Shampoo	Cleans human-hair wigs, hairpieces and hair additions
Mild Shampoo	Cleans synthetic wigs, hairpieces and hair additions
Synthetic Wig Shampoo	Cleans synthetic wigs, hairpieces and hair additions
Conditioner	Keeps wigs, hairpieces and hair additions in good condition
Synthetic Wig Conditioner	Keeps synthetic wigs, hairpieces and hair additions in optimum condition
Holding Spray	Holds finished human-hair wig, hairpiece and hair addition designs in place

WIG, HAIRPIECE AND HAIR ADDITION TOOLS AND SUPPLIES

TOOLS	FUNCTION
Comb	Detangles and styles wigs, hairpieces and hair additions
Brush	Styles wigs, hairpieces and hair additions
Shears	Shape and customize wigs, hairpieces and hair additions
Thinning Shears	Taper and blend; remove bulk and excess fiber
Razor	Tapers and blends; removes bulk and excess fiber
Rollers	Allow temporary curl placement for human-hair wigs and hairpieces
Clips	Attach hair additions to human-hair strands
J and L Color Ring	Allows client and salon professional to choose wig, hairpiece or hair addition color

SUPPLIES	FUNCTION
Wig Cap	Secures client's hair and keeps it flat
Bobby Pins	Secure client's hair under wig; sometimes used to hold wig in place
Hairpins	Secure hair, especially for chignons and other "updo" effects
Needle and Thread	Create darts and tucks in wigs; secure wefts in track-and-sew technique; used to sew wefts for fantasy hairpieces
Wig Pins	Hold wigs and hairpieces in place on canvas block during designing, cleaning and maintenance services
Styrofoam Heads	Store and display wigs
Chin Strap	Holds wig in place on client's head during services
Measuring Tape	Measures client's head to determine correct wig size
Plastic Bag	Covers and protects canvas blocks
Cloth Cape	Protects client during designing and fitting services
Hair Addition Fiber/Hair	Artificial hair, also called extensions, needed to perform hair addition services

WIG, HAIRPIECE AND HAIR ADDITION EQUIPMENT

EQUIPMENT	FUNCTION
Canvas Block (various sizes)	Holds wig while services are being performed
Wig Dryer	Dries human-hair wigs that have been wet-set (on canvas blocks)
Fusion Machine	Attaches hair additions to the client's hair
Hackle	A metal plate with rows of pointed needles used to blend or straighten fiber/hair during a hair addition service
Drawing Board	A flat mat used to hold hair extension fibers during a hair addition service

SALON**CONNECTION**

Donating Hair

In the future you might be approached by a client who asks you to help them donate their hair to make a wig for charitable purposes. It would be helpful for you to know some of the guidelines from these organizations.

>> The donated hair needs to be at least 8-10 inches measured tip to tip, which is the minimum length used for a hairpiece.

>> The donated hair must not be permed or color treated. (Check the organization's website.)

>> The hair must be in a ponytail or braid before it is cut.

>> The hair must be clean and completely dry before it is mailed in.

>> The ponytail or braid needs to be placed inside a plastic bag, and then inside an envelope.

Hopefully being familiar with these guidelines will help you and your client feel the reward of participating in such a worthy cause.

WIG, HAIRPIECE AND HAIR ADDITION INFECTION CONTROL AND SAFETY

It is essential to keep your client's safety in mind at all times. The majority of wig services are performed while the wig is on a wig block, so safety concerns are somewhat minimized. While applying hairpieces and hair additions, there are a few more concerns to keep in mind.

INFECTION CONTROL AND SAFETY – BEFORE THE SERVICE

>> Disinfect all tools, supplies, and equipment properly.

>> Use a fresh drape on every client.

>> Wash your hands with soap and warm water.

>> Check for allergic reaction to any adhesives used in the service by following manufacturer instructions for a patch test.

INFECTION CONTROL AND SAFETY – DURING THE SERVICE

>> Explain to your client points of maintenance and hygiene specific to each service.

>> Ensure that a wig or hairpiece has sufficient airflow if it will be worn for long periods of time.

>> Work with products, such as liquid dry shampoos, in a well-ventilated area.

>> Carefully observe the natural direction of hair growth when peforming a hair addition service; avoid going against the natural growth pattern, since doing so could cause discomfort to the client and damage to the hair.

INFECTION CONTROL AND SAFETY – AFTER THE SERVICE

>> Teach your clients how to maintain and care for any wig, hairpiece or hair addition.

- Although your artistry may make the wig, hairpiece or hair additions look like your clients' own hair, they cannot treat the additions in the exact same way.

>> Discard single-use supplies.

>> Clean and remove hair and debris from all tools and multi-use supplies prior to disinfection.

Wigs, hairpieces and hair additions can be a great additional skill that you can offer your clients. Besides the general products, tools and supplies listed in this lesson, it will be important to learn the essentials for the specific hair systems your salon offers. As these services are performed, it is also a necessity to keep the safety of your client in mind.

DISCOVER**MORE**

Here are just a few interesting facts about wigs. Research to find additional items you can share.

» Wolfgang Amadeus Mozart, one of the best known composers of the classical era, wore wigs for a definite purpose. He wanted to hide the deformity of his left ear.

» England's Queen Elizabeth I, the "Virgin Queen," owned over 150 wigs.

» A wig owned by Andy Warhol, famous painter and filmmaker, sold at auction for $10,800.

LESSONS LEARNED

Products, tools and supplies needed to perform wig, hairpiece and hair addition services include:

>> Nonflammable liquid shampoo, mild shampoo, synthetic wig shampoo

>> Conditioner, synthetic wig conditioner

>> Holding spray

>> Comb, brush, shears, thinning shears, razor

>> Rollers, pincurl clips, bobby pins, hairpins

>> Wig cap

>> Needle and thread, wig pins, styrofoam heads, chin strap

>> J and L Color Ring

>> Measuring tape

>> Plastic bag

>> Cloth tape

>> Hair addition fiber/hair

Equipment used in wig, hairpiece and hair addition services includes:

>> Various canvas blocks

>> Wig dryer

>> Brand-specific fusion machine for hair additions

>> Hackle

>> Drawing board

Infection control and safety concerns before, during and after a wig, hairpiece or hair addition service include:

>> Before – Disinfect all tools and equipment, use a fresh drape, wash hands. Ensure your client is not allergic to adhesives you may be using by following manufacturer patch test instructions.

>> During – Explain points of maintenance and hygiene, ensure that the wig or hairpiece has sufficient airflow, work in well-ventilated area, when performing a hair addition service pay close attention to natural growth patterns.

>> After – Inform your clients to maintain and care for any wig, hairpiece, or hair addition service.

>> Discard single-use supplies, clean and disinfect tools and multi-use supplies.

109^c GLOSSARY/INDEX

PIVOT POINT

ACKNOWLEDGMENTS

Pivot Point Fundamentals is designed to provide education to undergraduate students to help prepare them for licensure and an entry-level position in the cosmetology field. An undertaking of this magnitude requires the expertise and cooperation of many people who are experts in their field. Pivot Point takes pride in our internal team of educators who develop cosmetology, esthetics and nails education, along with our print and digital experts, designers, editors, illustrators and video producers. Pivot Point would like to express our many thanks to these talented individuals who have devoted themselves to the business of beauty, lifelong learning and especially for help raising the bar for future professionals in our industry.

EDUCATION DEVELOPMENT **Janet Fisher** // **Sabine Held-Perez** // **Vasiliki A. Stavrakis**
Markel Artwell
Eileen Dubelbeis
Brian Fallon
Melissa Holmes
Lisa Luppino
Paul Suttles
Amy Gallagher
Lisa Kersting
Jamie Nabielec
Vic Piccolotto
Ericka Thelin
Jane Wegner

EDITORIAL **Maureen Spurr** // **Wm. Bullion** // **Deidre Glover**
Liz Bagby
Jack Bernin
Lori Chapman

DESIGN & PRODUCTION **Jennifer Eckstein** // **Rick Russell** // **Danya Shaikh**
Joanna Jakubowicz
Denise Podlin
Annette Baase
Agnieszka Hansen
Kristine Palmer
Tiffany Wu

PROJECT MANAGEMENT **Jenny Allen** // **Ken Wegrzyn**

DIGITAL DEVELOPMENT John Bernin
Javed Fouch
Anna Fehr
Matt McCarthy
Marcia Noriega
Corey Passage
Herb Potzus

Pivot Point also wishes to take this opportunity to acknowledge the many contributors and product concept testers who helped make this program possible.

INDUSTRY CONTRIBUTORS

Linda Burmeister
Esthetics

Jeanne Braa Foster
Dr. Dean Foster
Eyes on Cancer

Mandy Gross
Nails

Andrea D. Kelly, MA, MSW
University of Delaware

Rosanne Kinley
Infection Control
National Interstate Council

Lynn Maestro
Cirépil by Perron Rigot, Paris

Andrzej Matracki
World and European
Men's Champion

MODERN SALON

Rachel Molepske
Look Good Feel Better, PBA
CUT IT OUT, PBA

Peggy Moon
Liaison to Regulatory and Testing

Robert Richards
Fashion Illustrations

Clif St. Germain, Ph.D
Educational Consultant

Andis Company

International Dermal Institute

HairUWear Inc.

Lock & Loaded Men's Grooming

PRODUCT CONCEPT TESTING

Central Carolina
Community College
Millington, North Carolina

Gateway Community Colleges
Phoenix, Arizona

MC College
Edmonton, Alberta

Metro Beauty Academy
Allentown, Pennsylvania

Rowan Cabarrus
Community College
Kannapolis, North Carolina

Sunstate Academy of
Cosmetology and Massage
Ft. Myers, Florida

The Salon Professional Academy
Kokomo, Indiana

TONI&GUY Hairdressing Academy
Costa Mesa, California
Plano, Texas

Xenon Academy
Omaha, NE
Grand Island, NE

LEADERSHIP TEAM

Robert Passage
Chairman and CEO

Robert J. Sieh
Senior Vice President,
Finance and Operations

Judy Rambert
Vice President, Education

Kevin Cameron
Senior Vice President,
Education and Marketing

R.W. Miller
Vice President, Domestic Sales
and Field Education

Jan Laan
Vice President, International
Business Development

Katy O'Mahony
Director, Human Resources

In addition, we give special thanks to the North American Regulating agencies whose careful work protects us as well as our clients, enhancing the high quality of our work. These agencies include Occupational Health and Safety Agency (OSHA) and the U.S. Environmental Protection Agency (EPA). *Pivot Point Fundamentals*™ promotes use of their policies and procedures.

Pivot Point International would like to express our SPECIAL THANKS to the inspired visual artisans of Creative Commons, without whose talents this book of beauty would not be possible.

#MOOD

get creative: write, sketch, collage your ideas here

goals:

_____

_____

_____

_____

_____

_____

_____

_____

_____

salons i like:

_____

_____

_____

_____

_____

_____

_____

_____

@pivotpointintl
#pivotpoint
#learnforward
#pivotpointcosmetology

#MOOD